I0617081

40 Days of Reflection,
Action, and Transformation

unshakable
growth

VINROY MORRISON JR.

VinroyMorrisonGroup.com

Copyright © 2025 Vinroy Morrison Jr.

All rights reserved.

Book Design by Jennifer Stimson

ISBN: 979-8-9929032-0-1 (Paperback)

ISBN: 979-8-9929032-1-8 (Ebook)

www.vinroymorrisongroup.com

Table of Contents

Introduction

Welcome to *Unshakable Growth: 40 Days of Reflection, Action, and Transformation*. This book is your companion on a journey of self-discovery, personal growth, and lasting transformation. Each day is designed to challenge your perspective, inspire intentional action, and guide you toward becoming the best version of yourself.

"Growth is not a destination; it's a lifelong process."

This devotional will help you explore your strengths, confront challenges, and embrace opportunities to change. Through reflection and action, you will plant seeds of transformation that, when nurtured, will create unshakable growth.

How to Use This Book:

1. Take It Day by Day: Dedicate time each day to reflect, take action, and engage with the prompts.
2. Stay Open and Honest: Be vulnerable with yourself—this is your space for growth.
3. Revisit Lessons Often: Transformation takes time, and the most meaningful insights often deepen with repetition.

At the heart of this journey is the belief that growth is unshakable when it's rooted in intention, action, and reflection. Let this devotional be your guide and companion as you pursue a life of purpose and fulfillment.

With encouragement,
Vinroy Morrison, Jr.

Your 40-Day
Journey Path Overview:

DAYS 1-10: LAYING THE FOUNDATION

Day 1: "Who Does It Matter To?"

- **REFLECTION:** Importance of identifying your audience.
- **ACTION STEPS:** Identify your audience, observe patterns, and align your energy.

Day 2: "Guard Your Words in Conflict"

- **REFLECTION:** The power of words in conflict.
- **ACTION STEPS:** Pause before speaking, focus on the issue, and practice restraint.

Day 3: "The Power of Authenticity"

- **REFLECTION:** Authenticity leads to fulfillment.

- **ACTION STEPS:** Identify your true self, let go of pretenses, and find your tribe.

Day 4: "The Right Environment for Growth"

- **REFLECTION:** The influence of surroundings.
- **ACTION STEPS:** Audit your environment, seek growth-oriented communities, and make necessary changes.

Day 5: "Adversity as a Mirror"

- **REFLECTION:** Using adversity for growth.
- **ACTION STEPS:** Reflect honestly, identify the lesson, and take action.

Day 6: "Investigate Before You Invest"

- **REFLECTION:** Importance of understanding before committing.
- **ACTION STEPS:** Do your research, ask clarifying questions, and seek understanding.

Day 7: "The Difference Between Being 'Grown' and Growing Up"

- **REFLECTION:** Maturity beyond appearances.
- **ACTION STEPS:** Self-check, commit to growth, and embrace humility.

Day 8: "Stand Up or Sit Out"

- **REFLECTION:** Active participation in life.
- **ACTION STEPS:** Define your game, take the first step, and commit to consistency.

Day 9: "Break the Cycle of Inconsistency"

- **REFLECTION:** Importance of consistency.
- **ACTION STEPS:** Identify patterns, set small, achievable goals, and track your progress.

Day 10: "Celebrate Without Stopping"

- **REFLECTION:** Balance between celebration and progress.
- **ACTION STEPS:** Celebrate with gratitude, set your next goal, stay humble and motivated.

DAYS 11-20: BUILDING MOMENTUM

Day 11: "Seize Your Moment"

- **REFLECTION:** Preparation increases readiness.
- **ACTION STEPS:** Define your window, prepare daily, and embrace the habit.

Day 12: "The Power of Identity and Purpose"

- **REFLECTION:** Alignment with identity and purpose.
- **ACTION STEPS:** Clarify your identity, define your purpose, and align your actions.

Day 13: "The Student's Journey"

- **REFLECTION:** Embrace lifelong learning.
- **ACTION STEPS:** Evaluate your teachers, seek meaning in every encounter, and apply what you learn.

Day 14: "The Power of Consistency"

- **REFLECTION:** Consistency as a force for success.
- **ACTION STEPS:** Commit to the process, track your progress, and embrace discipline.

Day 15: "The Art of Receiving Feedback"

- **REFLECTION:** Discernment in receiving feedback.
- **ACTION STEPS:** Evaluate the source, filter for value, respond, don't react.

Day 16: "Define Your Own Narrative"

- **REFLECTION:** Control over your story.
- **ACTION STEPS:** Own your story, filter feedback, and stay grounded.

Day 17: "Driven by Purpose, Not Hate"

- **REFLECTION:** Purpose as a positive motivator.
- **ACTION STEPS:** Identify your purpose, release hate, and sustain the drive.

Day 18: "Value the Journey"

- **REFLECTION:** Embrace the journey for transformation.
- **ACTION STEPS:** Embrace the process, celebrate small wins, and stay present.

Day 19: "Embracing Your Gift"

- **REFLECTION:** Recognizing and sharing your gifts.
- **ACTION STEPS:** Identify, cultivate, and share your gift.

Day 20: "Bringing Value Without Attachment"

- **REFLECTION:** Detaching from the need for validation.
- **ACTION STEPS:** Focus on contribution, detach from outcomes, and reflect on your efforts.

DAYS 21-30: DEEPENING UNDERSTANDING

Day 21: "Balancing Patience and Perseverance"

- **REFLECTION:** Finding balance in persistence.
- **ACTION STEPS:** Assess your balance, set milestones, and practice self-care.

Day 22: "The Power of Execution"

- **REFLECTION:** Execution is key to realizing vision.
- **ACTION STEPS:** Clarify your vision, take immediate action, and stay consistent.

Day 23: "Leveling Life's Struggles"

- **REFLECTION:** Embracing challenges as growth opportunities.
- **ACTION STEPS:** Identify struggles, develop a strategy, and celebrate progress.

Day 24: "Embracing Mixed Responses"

- **REFLECTION:** Accepting diverse opinions.
- **ACTION STEPS:** Expect variety, stay grounded, and filter feedback.

Day 25: "Leadership Through Vision"

- **REFLECTION:** Leading with clarity and authenticity.
- **ACTION STEPS:** Define your vision, model the way, and inspire others.

Day 26: "The Power of Consistency"

- **REFLECTION:** Standing out through consistency.
- **ACTION STEPS:** Identify key areas, create a plan, and track progress.

Day 27: "Peace with the Past"

- **REFLECTION:** Embracing peace for forward movement.
- **ACTION STEPS:** Reflect and release, learn the lessons, and focus forward.

Day 28: "Writing Your Success Story"

- **REFLECTION:** Shaping your life's narrative through choices.
- **ACTION STEPS:** Visualize your story, take control of the pen, and embrace revisions.

Day 29: "Focus on the Next Step"

- **REFLECTION:** Importance of small, intentional steps.
- **ACTION STEPS:** Identify your next step, take intentional action, reflect, and repeat.

Day 30: "Gifts and Character"

- **REFLECTION:** Sustaining success with character.
- **ACTION STEPS:** Evaluate your character, strengthen integrity, and let your character lead.

DAYS 31-40: EMBRACING CHANGE AND GROWTH

Day 31: "Letting Go of Bitterness"

- **REFLECTION:** Release bitterness for growth.
- **ACTION STEPS:** Acknowledge bitterness, practice forgiveness, and shift your focus.

Day 32: "The Power of Your Environment"

- **REFLECTION:** Environment as a growth catalyst.
- **ACTION STEPS:** Audit your environment, seek growth spaces, and be intentional.

Day 33: "The Value of Time"

- **REFLECTION:** Treat time as a valuable resource.
- **ACTION STEPS:** Audit your time, set priorities, and be intentional.

Day 34: "Your Story is Still Unfolding"

- **REFLECTION:** Embrace the ongoing nature of your story.
- **ACTION STEPS:** Reframe the past, embrace the present, and visualize the future.

Day 35: "The Power of Learning"

- **REFLECTION:** Learning as a key to possibilities.
- **ACTION STEPS:** Adopt a growth mindset, be willing to be challenged, and create a learning habit.

Day 36: "Know Your Worth, Show Your Value"

- **REFLECTION:** Confidence through understanding your worth.
- **ACTION STEPS:** Define your worth, show your value, and set boundaries.

Day 37: "Release the Identity of Pain"

- **REFLECTION:** Healing beyond pain identification.
- **ACTION STEPS:** Reflect on your identity, choose healing, and rewrite the narrative.

Day 38: "Refined by Pain, Not Defined by It"

- **REFLECTION:** Use pain for refinement.
- **ACTION STEPS:** Acknowledge the pain, embrace refinement, and release complaints.

Day 39: "Choose Healing Over Validation"

- **REFLECTION:** Healing as a transformative power.
- **ACTION STEPS:** Identify the patterns, embrace healing, and replace validation with growth.

Day 40: "Embrace the Present"

- **REFLECTION:** Living in the present moment.
- **ACTION STEPS:** Stop the chase, practice presence, and set realistic goals.

DAYS 1-10
Laying the Foundation

DAY 1
"Who Does It Matter To?"

QUOTE:

"STOP wasting your time telling people things that they don't care to know. What you have to say, share, vent about, etc., matters. You just have to know who it matters to."

REFLECTION:

Have you ever poured your heart out only to feel unheard or dismissed? It's a frustrating experience. But the problem isn't always in what you're saying—it's in who you're saying it to. Every message, idea, or emotion has an audience, and finding the right audience is key to being impactful.

Think about this: even the most powerful speech can fall flat if it's spoken to the wrong crowd. Your words have value, but their impact depends on finding ears that are ready to hear them.

ACTION STEPS:

- Identify your audience: Who truly values your voice? Reflect on the people who engage with your words or ideas and give thoughtful feedback.
- Observe patterns: Take note of situations where you've felt dismissed. What do those scenarios have in common?
- Align your energy: Focus your time and words on those who reciprocate your respect and attention.

REFLECTION PROMPT:

- Who in your life truly listens to you? Write down three people who value your perspective.
- What's one thing you've been holding back, and who might need to hear it?

DAY 2

"Guard Your Words in Conflict"

"Never defame the character of another because you may have a disagreement or a falling out, because if you both reconcile your friendship, those you've went to, defaming the character of the other person, may never see them in the same light again."

REFLECTION:

In moments of conflict, it's easy to let emotions take over and say things we later regret. But words have power—power to heal and power to harm. When we speak poorly of someone in the heat of the moment, we risk leaving a permanent mark on how others perceive them. Even if you reconcile, the damage to their reputation might remain in the minds of those who heard your words.

The true strength of character is shown in how we handle disagreements. Protecting the dignity of others, even when it's difficult, is a mark of maturity and respect.

ACTION STEPS:

- Pause Before Speaking: In moments of anger, take a moment to breathe and reflect. Ask yourself, "Will my words build up or tear down?"
- Focus on the Issue: Speak to the problem, not the person. Avoid personal attacks or harsh criticisms.
- Practice Restraint: If you need to vent, choose a trusted confidant who won't spread negativity. Be mindful of what you share and with whom.

REFLECTION PROMPT:

- Think about a time when you spoke negatively about someone during a disagreement. How could you have handled it differently?
- Who in your life can you trust to offer a listening ear without fueling conflict? Write their name down as your "go-to" in tense moments.

DAY 3
"The Power of Authenticity"

QUOTE:

"You can only be your true self! Pretending to be someone other than yourself to fit in will only let you fit in as long as you can keep not being who you really are!"

REFLECTION:

Authenticity is the key to lasting fulfillment. When we pretend to be someone we're not, we might achieve temporary acceptance, but at what cost? The effort to maintain a façade is exhausting, and it disconnects us from our true selves.

The world doesn't need another copy—it needs the unique voice and gifts that only you can bring. Fitting in is overrated; standing out as your authentic self is where the real magic happens.

ACTION STEPS:

- Identify Your True Self: Write down 3–5 qualities that define who you are at your core. What makes you unique? For example:
    1. Resilient – You've overcome significant obstacles and never give up.
    2. Empathetic – You deeply understand others' emotions and perspectives.
    3. Inquisitive – You always seek deeper meaning and understanding.
    4. Creative – You see the world differently and bring fresh ideas to life.
    5. Authentic – You value truth and express yourself honestly.

- Let Go of Pretenses: Reflect on areas of your life where you're trying to fit in. What changes can you make to show up as your true self?
- Find Your Tribe: Seek relationships and environments where you feel valued for who you truly are, not for who you think you need to be.

REFLECTION PROMPT:

- What parts of yourself have you been hiding to fit in? How can you start expressing them more fully?
- Who in your life accepts and loves you as you are? What can you learn from those relationships?

DAY 4

"The Right Environment for Growth"

QUOTE:

"There is a certain environment that's needed for your growth and fruition! Pay attention to your surroundings! If your surroundings don't promote maturity, growth, betterment, and the like, you need to make some changes."

REFLECTION:

Just like a plant needs the right soil, sunlight, and water to thrive, you need an environment that nurtures your growth. Your surroundings—physical, emotional, and relational—shape who you are becoming. If your current environment stifles your potential, it may be time to rethink where and with whom you invest your time.

Growth flourishes in spaces filled with encouragement, accountability, and challenge.

Ask yourself: Does your environment align with who you want to be?

ACTION STEPS:

- Audit Your Environment: Take an honest look at your physical spaces, relationships, and habits. Are they helping or hindering your growth?
- Seek Growth-Oriented Communities: Surround yourself with people who inspire and challenge you to be better.
- Make Necessary Changes: Remove or distance yourself from toxic influences. Start incorporating spaces, activities, and relationships that promote maturity and betterment. For example:

Before making meaningful progress, you must clear the path of toxic influences and intentionally create space for personal growth. Follow this guided reflection and action plan:

STEP 1: IDENTIFY TOXIC INFLUENCES

Ask yourself: What in my life drains my energy, holds me back, or fills me with negativity?

Write down three specific toxic influences that you need to remove or distance yourself from. These could be:

- A negative relationship (friend, colleague, or family member) that constantly discourages or belittles you.

- An unhealthy habit (excessive social media, procrastination, self-doubt).
- A toxic environment (a workplace, social circle, or even a mental space like constant comparison).

Example Response:

1. I have a friend who constantly criticizes my dreams and makes me doubt myself.
2. I spend too much time scrolling through social media, feeling like I'm not good enough.
3. My workplace is full of gossip and negativity, making it hard to stay positive.

STEP 2: TAKE ACTION TO REMOVE OR DISTANCE YOURSELF

Now, next to each toxic influence, write down one concrete step you can take to reduce its impact on your life.

Example Response:

1. I will set boundaries with my negative friend and limit our conversations. If they continue to discourage me, I'll prioritize relationships that uplift me.
2. I will set a daily 30-minute limit on social media and replace that time with journaling or reading.
3. I will create a positive mindset by listening to motivational podcasts during my commute and avoiding negative office gossip.

STEP 3: REPLACE WITH POSITIVE INFLUENCES

Now that you've cleared some space, it's time to intentionally add healthy, uplifting activities, environments, and relationships.

Ask yourself: What can I do daily to promote growth, maturity, and well-being?

Example Response:

- New Environment: I will spend more time at the library or coffee shops where I feel inspired to write.
- New Habit: I will replace mindless scrolling with reading one self-improvement book per month.
- New Relationships: I will join a writers' group or attend personal development events to connect with like-minded people.

STEP 4: COMMIT TO THE CHANGE

Write a short commitment statement to solidify your decision.

Example:

"I am committed to removing negativity from my life and surrounding myself with people and activities that inspire growth. I will take control of my environment, set boundaries, and be intentional about my personal development."

REFLECTION PROMPT:

- In what ways does your current environment support or hinder your growth?
- What is one change you can make this week to create a more growth-oriented environment?

DAY 5

"Adversity as a Mirror"

QUOTE:

"Maturing in one's character is to not allow pain or disappointments to enforce certain behaviors but rather to reveal any character flaws that you may have and addressing them accordingly."

REFLECTION:

Pain and disappointment are unavoidable in life. While it's natural to feel hurt, how you respond to these challenges determines your growth. Immaturity allows pain to dictate our behaviors, often leading to bitterness or self-sabotage. Maturity, however, sees adversity as a mirror, reflecting areas where growth is needed.

Instead of letting setbacks shape your actions, use them as opportunities to uncover and address character flaws. The result? A stronger, wiser, and more resilient you.

ACTION STEPS:

- Reflect Honestly: Think about a recent disappointment. What behaviors did it trigger in you? Were those behaviors constructive or destructive?
- Identify the Lesson: Ask yourself, "What is this situation teaching me about myself?" Look for patterns in your reactions.
- Take Action: Create a plan to address the flaws revealed by adversity. For example, if impatience was exposed, practice mindfulness or set boundaries to manage expectations.

REFLECTION PROMPT:

- What recent challenge has tested your character? What did it reveal about you?
- How can you use this insight to grow into the person you want to become?

DAY 6

"Investigate Before You Invest"

QUOTE:

"It's best to INVESTIGATE before you INVEST! Be sure to research, ask questions, and clarify before you make a decision! In all thy getting, get... UNDERSTANDING! I'm not saying you shouldn't make the move; I'm saying you should know what you're moving into!"

REFLECTION:

Every decision you make is an investment—of your time, energy, resources, or emotions. The quality of that investment often depends on the level of understanding you have beforehand. Rash decisions can lead to unnecessary setbacks, while thoughtful investigation can open doors to clarity and success.

In the rush to move forward, it's easy to skip the step of asking questions and gathering information. But wisdom says: slow down, do your homework, and ensure your choices align with your values and goals.

ACTION STEPS:

- Do Your Research: Before committing to a decision, gather all the necessary information. Read, ask questions, and seek expert advice.
- Ask Clarifying Questions: What are the potential risks? What is the expected return? Are you ready to commit the required time and energy?
- Seek Understanding: Reflect on how the decision aligns with your long-term vision. If it doesn't bring clarity or peace, pause and reassess.

REFLECTION PROMPT:

- Think of a recent decision you made quickly. Did it turn out as you expected?
- What steps can you take to be more thorough in your decision-making process going forward?

DAY 7

"The Difference Between Being 'Grown' and Growing Up"

QUOTE:

"Don't be so busy trying to be 'Grown' that you never Grow Up!"

REFLECTION:

Many people equate being "grown" with independence, success, or having responsibilities. But true maturity—growing up—is about wisdom, accountability, and emotional growth. You can handle adult responsibilities and still lack the self-awareness and discipline that come with real personal development.

Growing up means striving to be a better version of yourself daily, not just projecting the image of someone who has it all together. It's an internal transformation, not an external performance.

ACTION STEPS:

- Self-Check: Reflect on areas in your life where you might be focusing more on appearances than on substance.
- Commit to Growth: Identify one habit or mindset you need to let go of to grow emotionally or spiritually.
- Embrace Humility: Seek feedback from trusted mentors or friends on how you can mature in your character.

REFLECTION PROMPT:

- What does "being grown" mean to you? How does it differ from truly growing up?
- What is one area of your life where you could focus on deeper growth rather than surface-level maturity?

DAY 8

"Stand Up or Sit Out"

QUOTE:

"We're gonna either STAND on business or SIT on the bench! Benchwarmers don't get to play the game. They just get to watch from the sidelines."

REFLECTION:

Life isn't a spectator sport. If you're not actively pursuing your goals, advocating for yourself, and taking action, you risk being left on the sidelines. Success and growth come to those who are willing to step up, face challenges, and take risks.

Sitting on the bench may feel safe, but it robs you of the satisfaction and growth that comes from playing the game.

The question is: Are you willing to stand on your principles, face the pressure, and take action?

ACTION STEPS:

- Define Your Game: Identify the key area of your life where you need to step up. Is it your career, relationships, or personal growth?
- Take the First Step: What's one action you can take today to move off the sidelines and into the game?
- Commit to Consistency: Growth and success aren't about single plays—they're about showing up day after day.

REFLECTION PROMPT:

- What does it mean to you to "stand on business"?
- In what area of your life have you been sitting on the bench, and what's stopping you from stepping onto the field?

DAY 9

"Break the Cycle of Inconsistency"

QUOTE:

"Don't allow inconsistency to be the only thing you're consistent with!"

REFLECTION:

Inconsistency is the silent killer of dreams and progress. It's easy to start with good intentions but difficult to maintain the discipline needed for lasting success. When inconsistency becomes your default, it erodes trust—in yourself and others.

True growth comes from showing up, even when it's hard, inconvenient, or uncomfortable. Consistency builds momentum, and momentum creates transformation.

ACTION STEPS:

- Identify Patterns: What areas of your life suffer from inconsistency? Write them down and reflect on what causes the cycle to repeat.
- Set Small, Achievable Goals: Start with one area where consistency would have the most impact. Commit to showing up daily, even in small ways.
- Track Your Progress: Use a journal or habit tracker to celebrate wins and hold yourself accountable.

REFLECTION PROMPT:

- In what areas of your life have you been inconsistent? How has this affected your growth?
- What's one small action you can commit to today to start building consistency?

DAY 10
"Celebrate Without Stopping"

QUOTE:

"A 'Flex' is meant to showcase the dedication and effort you've invested in your pursuits. However, overdoing it or holding onto that moment for too long can lead to a cramp. Please remember to keep moving!"

REFLECTION:

It's natural to take pride in your accomplishments. After all, they represent your hard work, persistence, and growth. But the danger lies in lingering too long in celebration, allowing the momentum of progress to fade. Life is a journey, not a single destination.

True greatness comes from balancing moments of triumph with the drive to keep growing. Acknowledge your wins but stay focused on the path ahead.

ACTION STEPS:

- Celebrate with Gratitude: Take time to reflect on your accomplishments and thank those who supported you.
- Set Your Next Goal: After celebrating, identify the next milestone you want to reach. Keep your energy directed forward.
- Stay Humble and Motivated: Use your successes as motivation to continue striving rather than as a reason to pause indefinitely.

REFLECTION PROMPT:

- What recent accomplishment are you most proud of? How did you celebrate it?
- How can you use that success as fuel to pursue your next goal?

DAYS 11-20
Building Momentum

DAY 11
"Seize Your Moment"

QUOTE:

"READY TO SEIZE YOUR MOMENT? Consistently showing up increases your chances of seizing your 'window of opportunity' when it arrives! It also builds a good habit because once you seize the moment, you'll be ready for the next."

REFLECTION:

Opportunities don't often announce themselves—they arrive unexpectedly and are only visible to those who are prepared. The secret to success lies in consistently showing up, honing your skills, and staying ready. When your window of opportunity opens, your readiness will determine whether you can step through it or miss it.

Every moment you prepare strengthens the habit of showing up. This doesn't just help you seize one opportunity—it creates a cycle of readiness for all that life has to offer.

ACTION STEPS:

- Define Your Window: What is the opportunity you're hoping to seize? Be specific about your goals.
- Prepare Daily: Commit to consistent actions that align with your goals. Even small steps build momentum over time.
- Embrace the Habit: Reflect on how consistency in one area of your life can prepare you for growth in others.

REFLECTION PROMPT:

- What's one opportunity you've missed because you weren't ready? How can you ensure you're prepared next time?
- What habits can you build now to stay ready for your "window of opportunity"?

DAY 12

"The Power of Identity and Purpose"

QUOTE:

"Identity and Purpose are the two things that I love to speak to and resonate with me a lot! While the actions you take may vary, the essence of being your best self is what truly matters."

REFLECTION:

Your identity is who you are, and your purpose is why you're here. Together, they form the foundation for a meaningful and fulfilling life. While the paths you take may change, staying true to your essence—the core of who you are and what drives you—will keep you aligned.

The pursuit of identity and purpose is not about perfection but about authenticity. When you live with intention, you naturally inspire others and find fulfillment in the journey.

ACTION STEPS:

- Clarify Your Identity: Reflect on your values, strengths, and the qualities that define you. Write them down as a reminder of who you are.
- Define Your Purpose: Ask yourself, "What impact do I want to have on the world around me?"
- Align Your Actions: Review your daily habits and decisions. Are they moving you closer to your purpose or pulling you away from it?

REFLECTION PROMPT:

- How would you describe your identity in three words?
- What does living in alignment with your purpose look like for you?

DAY 13
"The Student's Journey"

QUOTE:

"Embrace the lifelong journey of being a STUDENT, but choose your TEACHERS wisely. Not everyone can guide you, yet every encounter offers a LESSON. Your knowledge and its application are your true assets."

REFLECTION:

Life is an endless classroom, and every experience presents an opportunity to learn. However, not all teachers are equal. Wisdom comes from discerning who and what you allow to shape your perspective. While some lessons are found in uplifting mentorship, others are discovered in challenges or even mistakes.

True learning doesn't stop at acquiring knowledge—it's in applying that knowledge to better yourself and those around you. A wise student remains open, humble, and selective.

ACTION STEPS:

- Evaluate Your Teachers: Reflect on the people and experiences influencing you. Are they helping you grow or holding you back?
- Seek Meaning in Every Encounter: Even difficult situations can teach valuable lessons. Ask yourself, "What can I learn from this?"
- Apply What You Learn: Knowledge without action is wasted. Turn insights into tangible steps that enhance your life.

REFLECTION PROMPT:

- Who has been the most impactful teacher in your life? Why?
- What recent experience taught you an unexpected lesson, and how did it shape you?

DAY 14

"The Power of Consistency"

QUOTE:

"Consistency is the relentless force that propels you beyond the reach of your competitors, ensuring your enduring success in a dynamic world."

REFLECTION:

In a fast-changing world, many people start strong but struggle to sustain their efforts. The difference between fleeting success and lasting impact is consistency. It's the quiet, steady force that builds momentum, strengthens your skills, and sets you apart from the crowd.

Consistency isn't glamorous, but it's powerful. By showing up day after day, you create a foundation that can weather challenges and adapt to change.

Over time, small, consistent efforts yield extraordinary results.

ACTION STEPS:

- Commit to the Process: Identify one area of your life where consistency would make the greatest impact. Create a plan to stick with it, even when progress feels slow.
- Track Your Progress: Keep a journal or log to measure your efforts and celebrate milestones along the way.
- Embrace Discipline: Remind yourself that consistency is not about perfection; it's about perseverance. Focus on progress over time.

REFLECTION PROMPT:

- In what area of your life could consistency help you achieve greater success?
- What small action can you commit to every day to build momentum?

DAY 15

"The Art of Receiving Feedback"

QUOTE:

"Acknowledging that not all feedback will be positive or constructive is crucial. Sometimes, individuals might attempt to undermine you under the guise of providing honest feedback. Therefore, discernment is key."

REFLECTION:

Feedback is a powerful tool for growth, but not all of it comes from a place of truth or good intentions. Some feedback may be rooted in jealousy, misunderstanding, or even an attempt to discourage you. And on the flip side, some feedback could also not be helpful simply because it comes from someone who may not understand the issue at hand well; therefore, their feedback is misplaced, even if well-intentioned. That's why discernment is essential.

Learn to differentiate between constructive criticism that helps you grow and unhelpful feedback that distracts or diminishes you. The key is to stay open to learning while protecting your peace and confidence.

ACTION STEPS:

- Evaluate the Source: Consider the credibility and intentions of the person offering feedback. Are they invested in your growth, or is there another motive?
- Filter for Value: Ask yourself, "Does this feedback align with my goals or offer a perspective I hadn't considered?"
- Respond, Don't React: Practice gratitude for feedback, even if you choose not to act on it. Stay grounded and focus on your vision.

REFLECTION PROMPT:

- How do you typically respond to negative feedback? How can you approach it more effectively?
- Think of a piece of feedback you received recently. Was it constructive, and how did you handle it?

DAY 16

"Define Your Own Narrative"

QUOTE:

"Always Remember: Reading a book doesn't guarantee comprehension of its story. Many prefer summaries over truly grasping the character. Hence, while sometimes valuable, irrelevant feedback should not define your narrative."

REFLECTION:

People often form opinions about your life based on fragments of your story. They may skim the surface without truly understanding your journey, challenges, or intentions. It's important to remember that their perceptions, while occasionally insightful, do not define who you are.

Your story is unique, and it's yours to tell. Stay true to your character and purpose, even when others misunderstand or oversimplify your narrative. Growth comes from internal alignment, not external validation.

ACTION STEPS:

- Own Your Story: Reflect on what defines your character and values. Write them down as a personal guide.
- Filter Feedback: When receiving feedback, ask yourself, "Does this align with my values and goals?" If not, let it go.
- Stay Grounded: Remind yourself that others' opinions are often shaped by their own perspectives, not your truth.

REFLECTION PROMPT:

- How have others' opinions influenced your decisions in the past? How can you reclaim control of your narrative?
- What is one area of your life where you need to trust your own understanding over others' interpretations?

DAY 17
"Driven by Purpose, Not Hate"

QUOTE:

"Hate doesn't fuel my drive; purpose does. If hate fueled me, hate would have to sustain me. Hate is toxic to the heart and will cause rigor mortis and stagnation of the heart where you may never heal."

REFLECTION:

When hate becomes the driving force, it poisons the heart and stunts growth. Purpose, on the other hand, offers renewable energy that empowers and heals. Aligning your actions with purpose not only fuels your ambitions but also sustains them with meaning and clarity. Hate burns out quickly, leaving destruction in its path. Purpose builds, creating a foundation for enduring success and fulfillment.

ACTION STEPS:

- Identify Your Purpose: Reflect on what truly drives you. Write down the reasons behind your goals and ensure they align with your values.
- Release Hate: Let go of resentment and focus on positive motivations. Forgiveness and understanding are essential for healing and growth. I know this can be hard so I've included an example that you can adopt and work with.

Example:

Letting Go of Resentment & Focusing on Positive Motivation

STEP 1: IDENTIFY THE RESENTMENT

Think of one situation or person that has caused you frustration, disappointment, or hurt. Ask yourself:

- What am I holding onto?
- How does this resentment affect my emotions and actions?

Example:

"I feel resentful toward my former boss because they never appreciated my hard work and promoted someone else instead of me."

STEP 2: REFRAME YOUR PERSPECTIVE

Instead of letting resentment hold you back, ask:

- What can I learn from this?
- How can I turn this into motivation?

Example:

"Maybe this experience is pushing me to recognize my own worth and take control of my future. Instead of waiting for others to acknowledge me, I can focus on building skills and creating new opportunities for myself."

STEP 3: REPLACE RESENTMENT WITH POSITIVE MOTIVATION

Find a constructive action that channels your energy into growth instead of negativity.

Example:

"Instead of staying bitter about my old job, I'll focus on improving my skills and applying for roles where I feel valued. I'll use this as motivation to create a career that fulfills me."

STEP 4: LET GO & MOVE FORWARD

Write a short affirmation or commitment to remind yourself to release resentment and embrace positive action.

Example:

"I release my resentment because it no longer serves me. I choose to focus on my growth, happiness, and success."

- Sustain the Drive: Create daily habits that align with your purpose, reminding yourself of your "why" whenever challenges arise.

REFLECTION PROMPT:

- What motivates you to pursue your goals? Is it purpose or something less sustainable?

- How can you replace feelings of resentment or negativity with purpose-driven actions?

DAY 18
"Value the Journey"

QUOTE:

"Avoid being excessively focused on your goals to the point that you overlook the journey! It's not solely about reaching a destination but transforming into a better version of yourself."

REFLECTION:

Goals give us direction, but the journey shapes who we become. When we fixate solely on the destination, we miss out on the lessons, growth, and experiences along the way. Every step, whether challenging or rewarding, is part of the transformation. Remember, life isn't just about achieving milestones—it's about evolving into the best version of yourself through the process.

ACTION STEPS:

- Embrace the Process: Reflect daily on what you've learned or experienced rather than focusing solely on what's left to achieve.
- Celebrate Small Wins: Acknowledge and appreciate progress, no matter how small.
- Stay Present: Practice mindfulness to fully engage in each moment of the journey.

REFLECTION PROMPT:

- How has your journey so far shaped you into who you are today?
- What's one lesson or moment you've overlooked while chasing a goal?

DAY 19

"Embracing Your Gift"

QUOTE:

"When the gifted know they're gifted, they become the gift."

REFLECTION:

Everyone has unique talents and abilities, but true power comes from recognizing and embracing them. When you understand your gift, you not only enhance your own life but also become a source of inspiration and impact for others. Being the gift means sharing your talents with purpose, humility, and confidence. It's not about arrogance—it's about living in alignment with who you were created to be.

ACTION STEPS:

- Identify Your Gift: Reflect on your strengths and passions. What do you excel at, and how can you use it to help others?

- Cultivate Your Gift: Invest time in developing your gift and your abilities. Growth requires effort and intention.
- Share Your Gift: Look for ways to use your talents to uplift and inspire those around you.

REFLECTION PROMPT:

- What is one gift or talent you've recognized in yourself? How are you using it?
- How can you further develop and share your gift with the world?

DAY 20

"Bringing Value Without Attachment"

QUOTE:

"Your role is to bring value. Their role is to receive and act on it. If they don't accept or implement what's given, don't take it personally. Your value doesn't diminish by their lack of acknowledgment."

REFLECTION:

Your purpose is to add value through your words, actions, and presence. But the way others respond to that value is beyond your control. Some may embrace it, while others may overlook or reject it. True confidence comes from knowing that your worth isn't defined by others' recognition. Focus on doing your part wholeheartedly and trust that your efforts matter, even if their impact isn't immediately visible.

ACTION STEPS:

- Focus on Your Contribution: Concentrate on delivering value in everything you do without fixating on others' reactions.
- Detach from Outcomes: Remind yourself that your worth is independent of external validation.
- Reflect on Your Efforts: Regularly assess how you're adding value and adjust your approach to align with your goals.

REFLECTION PROMPT:

- How do you react when your efforts go unrecognized?
- How can you shift your mindset to remain confident in your value?
- What's one way you can bring value to someone's life today without expecting anything in return?

DAYS 21-30
Deepening Understanding

DAY 21

"Balancing Patience and Perseverance"

QUOTE:

"Patience serves as your steady anchor, keeping you grounded in the journey, while perseverance fuels your drive to move forward. Excessive patience can lead to complacency, while relentless perseverance without patience can lead to burnout."

REFLECTION:

Success requires both patience and perseverance, but finding the right balance is key. Patience helps you stay grounded and accept that progress takes time. Perseverance, on the other hand, drives you to keep pushing forward. Too much patience can stall momentum, while unchecked perseverance can drain your energy. The harmony between these two qualities creates a sustainable path to achieving your goals.

ACTION STEPS:

- Assess Your Balance: Reflect on whether you lean more toward patience or perseverance. Adjust where needed to maintain equilibrium.
- Set Milestones: Break your goal into smaller, achievable steps to track progress while staying motivated.
- Practice Self-Care: Build in time for rest and reflection to avoid burnout from relentless effort.

REFLECTION PROMPT:

- Are you more patient or perseverant in your current goals?
- How does this affect your progress?
- What's one way you can find a balance between staying grounded and pushing forward?

DAY 22
"The Power of Execution"

QUOTE:

"You'll either execute (carry out) the vision or execute (put to death) the vision! Either way, you're going to execute. It's up to you to determine which one you'll do! Execution is inevitable."

REFLECTION:

Every dream, idea, or goal requires action. Execution determines whether your vision thrives or fades away. The choice lies in how you direct your energy toward making the vision a reality or letting it slip into obscurity. Execution isn't optional; it's a natural consequence of time and decision-making. What matters is the intention and effort behind it. Decide to nurture your vision and bring it to life.

ACTION STEPS:

- Clarify Your Vision: Write down your goals and break them into actionable steps.
- Take Immediate Action: Don't wait for the "perfect" moment. Start with one step you can take today.
- Stay Consistent: Commit to regular progress. Small, consistent actions lead to big results over time.

REFLECTION PROMPT:

- What vision or goal have you been delaying?
- How can you start executing it today?
- What habits can you build to ensure your vision is carried out and not abandoned?

DAY 23
"Leveling Life's Struggles"

QUOTE:

*"There's a struggle on every level in life. So, in life,
we have to learn how to level every struggle."*

REFLECTION:

Life presents challenges at every stage, and with growth often comes new struggles. The key to thriving isn't avoiding difficulty but learning how to manage it effectively. Each struggle holds a lesson, and leveling up means developing the resilience and wisdom to overcome obstacles. By embracing struggles as opportunities for growth, you can transform challenges into stepping stones.

ACTION STEPS:

- Identify Your Struggles: Reflect on the current challenges you're facing. Write them down to gain clarity.
- Develop a Strategy: Break down each struggle into smaller, manageable tasks. Address them one step at a time.
- Celebrate Progress: Recognize and appreciate your growth after overcoming each challenge.

REFLECTION PROMPT:

- What is one struggle you've faced recently? How did it shape you?
- How can you approach your next challenge with a growth mindset?

DAY 24

"Embracing Mixed Responses"

QUOTE:

*"Go on ANY post and run through the comments!
I guarantee you will always see mixed opinions on
whatever you're looking at. If you want to be seen, heard,
or impactful, prepare your mind for mixed responses."*

REFLECTION:

In a world of diverse perspectives, mixed opinions are inevitable. The more visible or impactful you become, the more varied the responses you'll receive. The key is to stay true to your values and purpose, filtering feedback without letting it derail your progress. Remember, even polarizing reactions mean you're making an impact. Accept the mixed responses as part of your journey and focus on those who genuinely resonate with your message.

ACTION STEPS:

- Expect Variety: Anticipate a range of reactions to your ideas, and don't let negative ones discourage you.
- Stay Grounded: Revisit your "why" to stay focused on your purpose rather than external opinions.
- Filter Feedback: Accept constructive criticism and let go of unhelpful or irrelevant negativity.

REFLECTION PROMPT:

- How do you typically respond to criticism or mixed opinions?
- How can you improve your reaction?
- What is one step you can take to remain confident in your impact, even amidst diverse feedback?

DAY 25

"Leadership Through Vision"

QUOTE:

"You can't be an effective leader doing what everyone else does. You must personify the vision until they can see it and align themselves accordingly."

REFLECTION:

True leadership isn't about following the crowd—it's about standing out with clarity and conviction. As a leader, you must embody the vision you're striving for, serving as an example that inspires others to align with the goal. People follow what they can see and trust; it's up to you to be the embodiment of that vision. By staying authentic and purpose-driven, you create a path others are eager to follow.

ACTION STEPS:

- Define Your Vision: Write down the purpose and direction of your leadership. Be specific about what you stand for.
- Model the Way: Live in alignment with your vision. Let your actions reflect your goals and values.
- Inspire Others: Communicate your vision clearly and passionately to help others see their role in it.

REFLECTION PROMPT:

- What is the vision you want to lead others toward? How are you embodying it?
- How can you adjust your leadership style to inspire more trust and alignment?

DAY 26

"The Power of Consistency"

QUOTE:

"Sometimes, the ONE thing that makes you stand out from another is CONSISTENCY! That can also be the ONE thing that holds you back if you lack it."

REFLECTION:

Consistency is a defining factor between success and stagnation. It's not about being the most talented or having the best resources—it's about showing up, day after day, and doing the work. Small, steady efforts compound over time to create extraordinary results. On the flip side, inconsistency disrupts momentum and holds you back from achieving your potential. The choice to commit to consistency can make all the difference.

ACTION STEPS:

- Identify Key Areas: Reflect on where consistency could have the greatest impact on your life.
- Create a Plan: Set clear, achievable goals with a daily or weekly routine to maintain consistency.
- Track Progress: Use a journal or app to monitor your efforts and celebrate milestones along the way.

REFLECTION PROMPT:

- In what area of your life could greater consistency help you excel?
- What's one small action you can take daily to build consistency?

DAY 27

"Peace with the Past"

"A person who finds peace with their past is one who is unstoppable."

REFLECTION:

Your past shapes you, but it doesn't define you. Finding peace with your history—whether it's triumphs, mistakes, or pain—frees you from being weighed down by regret or bitterness. This peace empowers you to move forward with clarity and purpose, unshackled by the things you cannot change. When you embrace your past as part of your growth, you become unstoppable. You're no longer looking backward—you're focused on the limitless possibilities ahead.

ACTION STEPS:

- Reflect and Release: Identify areas of your past that still hold emotional weight. Practice forgiveness, both for yourself and others.
- Learn the Lessons: Consider what your experiences have taught you and how they've shaped your growth.
- Focus Forward: Set a goal that excites you and channel your energy into creating your future.

REFLECTION PROMPT:

- What part of your past have you struggled to make peace with?
- How can you take a step toward healing?
- How has your past prepared you for the person you're becoming?

DAY 28

"Writing Your Success Story"

QUOTE:

"You are working on your success story!
It's up to you how you fill in the blanks!"

REFLECTION:

Your life is a story in progress, and every choice you make shapes its direction. The power to fill in the blanks lies in your hands. Will you write a story of perseverance, growth, and purpose? Or will you let fear or doubt dictate the narrative? By intentionally choosing your actions and mindset, you can create a story that reflects the person you aspire to be.

ACTION STEPS:

- Visualize Your Story: Reflect on the legacy you want to create. What chapters are missing, and how can you write them?

- Take Control of the Pen: Make deliberate choices that align with your goals and values.
- Embrace Revisions: Don't be afraid to rewrite parts of your story. Growth comes from learning and adapting.

REFLECTION PROMPT:

- What does your success story look like so far?
- What chapters would you like to add?
- How can you start filling in the blanks with intentionality and purpose?

DAY 29
"Focus on the Next Step

QUOTE:

"Don't be so caught up looking for the final product/ destination that you miss the next step. We can lower our chances of a misstep if we focus on the next step."

REFLECTION:

It's natural to dream of the destination, but the journey is built one step at a time. Over-focusing on the end goal can cause you to overlook the small, intentional actions that lead there. Each step matters and lays the groundwork for progress. By staying present and focusing on the immediate next step, you create clarity and reduce unnecessary mistakes. Success is a series of well-taken steps, not just a single leap.

ACTION STEPS:

- Identify Your Next Step: Reflect on what you can do today to move closer to your goal.
- Take Intentional Action: Commit to completing that step with focus and care.
- Reflect and Repeat: After each step, assess your progress and determine the next actionable move.

REFLECTION PROMPT:

- What is one goal you've been focusing on?
- What's the very next step you can take toward it?
- How can you ensure that you remain present in the process?

DAY 30
"Gifts and Character"

QUOTE:

"Gifts Elevate! Character Validate! It's one thing for someone to trust your GIFTS; it's another thing for someone to trust YOU!"

REFLECTION:

Your gifts and talents can open doors and create opportunities, but it's your character that sustains them. People may be impressed by what you can do, but they'll only truly trust you if your actions align with integrity and authenticity. Character is the foundation of long-term success and meaningful relationships. It validates your gifts and makes your impact lasting.

ACTION STEPS:

- Evaluate Your Character: Reflect on whether your actions consistently align with your values.

- Strengthen Integrity: Make a conscious effort to keep your commitments and treat others with respect.
- Let Character Lead: Use your gifts to serve others, ensuring your impact is built on trust and authenticity.

REFLECTION PROMPT:

- How do your character and gifts complement each other?
- What is one way you can strengthen your character while using your gifts?

DAYS 31-40

Embracing Change and Growth

DAY 31
"Letting Go of Bitterness"

QUOTE:

"It's hard to get better if you're too busy staying bitter."

REFLECTION:

Bitterness is a heavy weight that holds you back from growth and healing. When you focus on past hurts, you limit your ability to move forward and become better. Letting go of bitterness frees up emotional energy to focus on progress and self-improvement.

True growth begins with forgiveness—of others and yourself. By releasing resentment, you create space for positivity and transformation.

ACTION STEPS:

- Acknowledge Bitterness: Reflect on areas where resentment may be lingering and holding you back.

- Practice Forgiveness: Let go of the need for retribution and focus on freeing yourself from emotional baggage. Once again, I know this is hard for many of us so I'm providing an example on how we can accomplish this.

HOW TO PRACTICE FORGIVENESS

Forgiveness isn't about excusing someone's actions—it's about freeing yourself from the emotional weight of resentment. Here's how you can do it:

1. Acknowledge Your Pain

Ask yourself: What hurt me? Why am I still holding onto it?
- Write down the situation or person that caused you pain.
- Recognize how it has affected you emotionally and mentally.

Example:

> *"I feel hurt because my close friend betrayed my trust. This has made me feel unworthy of true friendship."*

2. Shift Your Perspective

Instead of focusing on what was done to you, ask:
- Did this person act out of their own pain, ignorance, or limitations?
- What can I learn from this experience?

Example:

> *"Maybe my friend acted out of insecurity or fear. Their actions don't define my worth."*

3. Make a Conscious Choice to Let Go

Forgiveness is a decision you make for your own peace, not for the other person.

- Say to yourself (or write it down):

"I choose to release this pain because holding onto it only hurts me."

- If necessary, set boundaries to protect yourself in the future.

4. Replace Resentment with Healing Actions

Instead of dwelling on past hurt, focus on positive actions:
- Practice self-care and do things that bring you joy.
- Surround yourself with supportive people.
- Channel your emotions into something productive (journaling, exercise, creative expression).

Example:

*"I will focus on building healthier friendships
with people who value and respect me."*

5. Affirm Your Freedom

Forgiveness is about reclaiming your peace. Remind yourself daily:

*"I am free from the weight of resentment. I
choose healing, peace, and growth."*

- Shift Your Focus: Redirect your energy toward self-improvement and achieving your goals.

REFLECTION PROMPT:

- What is one area of your life where bitterness may be holding you back?
- How can you take steps to release it and focus on your growth?

DAY 32

"The Power of Your Environment"

QUOTE:

"Surround yourself with change and allow yourself to become what you behold. If your environment isn't conducive to change, it will induce the same behaviors, mindsets, and perspectives that keep you stagnant."

REFLECTION:

Your environment plays a critical role in shaping your mindset, actions, and growth. Being surrounded by inspiration, progress, and positive influences encourages you to evolve. Conversely, staying in an unchanging or toxic environment can hold you back.

To reach your full potential, you must actively choose environments that challenge and uplift you. Change begins when you allow yourself to grow beyond what's familiar.

ACTION STEPS:

- Audit Your Environment: Evaluate whether your surroundings and relationships promote growth or reinforce stagnation.
- Seek Growth Spaces: Identify and immerse yourself in environments that inspire and challenge you.
- Be Intentional: Regularly assess the influence of your environment and make changes as needed to align with your goals.

REFLECTION PROMPT:

- How is your current environment influencing your growth?
- What steps can you take to surround yourself with positive change?

DAY 33
"The Value of Time"

"Time is money where all sales are final!"

REFLECTION:

Time is one of the most valuable resources we have. Unlike money, it cannot be earned back or refunded once spent. Every moment carries an opportunity cost, and how you use your time determines the outcomes you achieve. Treat it as a precious commodity, investing it wisely and purposefully.

The finality of time makes every second an opportunity to build, grow, and create.

ACTION STEPS:

• Audit Your Time: Reflect on how you spend your days and identify areas where time might be wasted.

- Set Priorities: Focus on activities that align with your goals and values.
- Be Intentional: Plan your time carefully, treating it with the same importance as financial investments.

REFLECTION PROMPT:

- How are you currently spending your time, and does it align with your goals?
- What changes can you make to ensure you're using your time wisely?

DAY 34
"Your Story is Still Unfolding"

QUOTE:

"Don't mistake an old story for the whole story."

REFLECTION:

It's easy to let past experiences define your present and future. However, your life is a dynamic, ongoing story, and no single chapter represents the entire narrative. Growth happens when you embrace the truth that you are not bound by what has already occurred.

Your future holds infinite possibilities. By acknowledging the past without being defined by it, you open the door to new opportunities and transformation.

ACTION STEPS:

- Reframe the Past: Reflect on an old story or belief that no longer serves you. How can you rewrite it to align with your current vision?
- Embrace the Present: Focus on the chapter you're writing today. What choices can you make now to shape your future?
- Visualize the Future: Imagine the story you want to tell years from now. Start taking steps to make it a reality.

REFLECTION PROMPT:

- What "old story" have you been holding onto?
- How has it shaped your perspective?
- How can you begin to rewrite your narrative and embrace the whole story?

DAY 35
"The Power of Learning"

QUOTE:

*"Your ability to learn expands your possibilities, while
your willingness to learn narrows your limitations."*

REFLECTION:

Learning is the key to growth, transformation, and unlocking new opportunities. While the capacity to learn opens doors to endless possibilities, it's the willingness to embrace learning that removes the barriers holding you back.

When you approach life with curiosity and an open mind, you transform challenges into lessons and limitations into stepping stones.

ACTION STEPS:

- Adopt a Growth Mindset: Seek opportunities to learn from every experience, especially setbacks.
- Be Willing to Be Challenged: Embrace discomfort as a sign that you're growing beyond your current limits.
- Create a Learning Habit: Dedicate time daily or weekly to acquiring new skills, reading, or reflecting on your experiences.

REFLECTION PROMPT:

- What is one skill or area of knowledge you've been hesitant to explore?
- How can you cultivate a willingness to learn and overcome a current limitation?

DAY 36

Know Your Worth, Show Your Value

QUOTE:

"Know your worth; show your value."

REFLECTION:

Understanding your worth is the foundation of confidence and self-respect. When you truly know your worth, you set boundaries, make empowered decisions, and refuse to settle for less than you deserve.

Showing your value is about taking action—sharing your skills, talents, and contributions with the world. It's not about seeking validation but demonstrating your impact through tangible results and authenticity.

ACTION STEPS:

- Define Your Worth: Write down your strengths, talents, and qualities that make you unique.
- Show Your Value: Identify one area where you can actively demonstrate your skills or contributions.
- Set Boundaries: Say "no" to situations or opportunities that don't align with your worth or values.

REFLECTION PROMPT:

- How do you currently perceive your worth? Are there ways you could better align your actions with your values?
- What's one way you can show your value in your personal or professional life today?

DAY 37
Release the Identity of Pain

QUOTE:

*"When you identify yourself by your pain,
healing becomes your enemy."*

REFLECTION:

Pain is an inevitable part of life, but it is not who you are. When you define yourself by your pain, it can become a barrier to growth and healing. You may hold on to the hurt as a part of your identity, making it difficult to let go and move forward.

Healing requires releasing the attachment to the pain and embracing the possibility of freedom and renewal.

Ask yourself: Are you holding on to pain as a way of defining your story, or are you ready to create a new one? What if you can still tell your story but from a healed place?

ACTION STEPS:

- Reflect on Your Identity: Consider areas where you've allowed pain to shape your self-view. Write down how it has influenced your choices.
- Choose Healing: Identify one way you can prioritize healing, such as therapy, self-care, or forgiveness.
- Rewrite the Narrative: Replace the identity tied to pain with one centered on growth and resilience. For example, shift from "I'm a victim" to "I'm a survivor."

REFLECTION PROMPT:

- What aspects of your pain have become part of your identity?
- How can you release the attachment to pain and embrace healing as a friend rather than an enemy?

DAY 38

Refined by Pain, Not Defined by It

QUOTE:

"Don't let pain define you. If anything, let it refine you. We can complain about how unfair it is, but complaining doesn't change the fact that we've experienced or are experiencing it. Learn from it, but don't be bound by it. And please, don't be tied to it."

REFLECTION:

Pain is a teacher, not a permanent identity. Complaining about pain may provide temporary relief, but it doesn't bring transformation. Growth happens when you allow pain to refine you—shaping your character, resilience, and wisdom.

Reflect on how you've responded to pain in the past. Have you allowed it to make you stronger, or has it held you captive?

How can you shift your perspective to embrace the lessons pain has to offer?

ACTION STEPS:

- Acknowledge the Pain: Write down a painful experience and identify what it has taught you.
- Embrace Refinement: Reflect on one area where pain has strengthened your character or perspective.
- Release Complaints: For one week, commit to reframing complaints about pain into reflections on its lessons.

REFLECTION PROMPT:

- How has pain refined you rather than defined you?
- What is one lesson you've learned from a recent or past experience of pain, and how can you apply it today?

DAY 39

Choose Healing
Over Validation

*"Don't allow your pain to validate what
your healing should eradicate."*

REFLECTION:

Sometimes, pain can become a crutch, a way to justify holding on to habits, perspectives, or behaviors that healing seeks to remove. While it's important to honor your pain, clinging to it can prevent the very healing you need.

Healing requires letting go of the need for validation through pain and embracing the freedom that comes with release.

Ask yourself: Are you using your pain to justify staying the same, or are you allowing healing to transform you?

ACTION STEPS:

- Identify the Patterns: Reflect on areas in your life where pain has validated unhealthy habits or thought processes.
- Embrace Healing: Write down one area where you need healing and commit to taking an action step toward it (e.g., therapy, journaling, or open conversations).
- Replace Validation with Growth: Replace statements like "I act this way because of my pain" with affirmations like "I'm learning to heal and grow beyond this."

REFLECTION PROMPT:

- What habits or behaviors has your pain validated that healing can transform?
- How can you take a step toward letting healing replace pain as the driving force in your life?

DAY 40
Embrace the Present

QUOTE:

*"Playing 'Catch Up' only forfeits the current
moment, trying to chase what once was."*

REFLECTION:

Living in a mindset of "catching up" keeps you tethered to the past and prevents you from fully engaging with the present. The time and energy spent chasing what you think you've lost could be redirected toward building something meaningful right now.

Ask yourself: Are you trying to recreate the past, or are you ready to embrace the opportunities of today? The present moment holds the power to shape your future if you choose to focus on it.

ACTION STEPS:

- Stop the Chase: Identify an area where you feel like you're "behind" and shift your focus to what you can do today.
- Practice Presence: Set aside 10 minutes daily to be fully present, whether through mindfulness, journaling, or simply observing your surroundings.
- Set Realistic Goals: Instead of chasing the past, create one actionable goal that aligns with where you are now and moves you forward.

REFLECTION PROMPT:

- In what areas of your life do you feel like you're "catching up"?
- How can you let go of what was and embrace what is?

CONCLUSION
Your Journey Continues!

As you close this devotional, reflect on the growth and insights you've cultivated over these 40 days. Each entry was designed to challenge your perspective, inspire action, and lead you closer to becoming the best version of yourself. Growth is not a destination; it's a lifelong journey.

You've explored your strengths, confronted challenges, and embraced opportunities for change. These moments of reflection and action are the seeds of transformation. Continue to nurture them daily by staying curious, intentional, and open to learning.

Key Takeaways:

- Embrace Progress Over Perfection: Each small step you take matters. Celebrate every victory, no matter how small. Growth happens one moment at a time.
- Stay Aligned With Your Purpose: Let your values and vision guide your decisions. A life lived on purpose is a life of fulfillment.
- Remain Resilient: Challenges are inevitable, but they are also opportunities to refine your character and strengthen your resolve.

Looking Forward:

Take the lessons you've learned and integrate them into your daily life. Revisit the entries and prompts that resonated most deeply and use them as touchstones when you face new challenges. Share your journey with others, inspiring them to pursue their own growth.

Final Reflection Prompt:

- What have you learned about yourself through this journey?
- How can you commit to ongoing growth in the months and years ahead?

Your growth is unshakable when it's rooted in intention, action, and reflection. Carry this truth forward with confidence and courage as you continue to transform your life.

Thank you for allowing this devotional to be a part of your journey.

With gratitude and encouragement,
Vinroy Morrison Jr.

www.ingramcontent.com/pod-product-compliance
Lightning Source LLC
Chambersburg PA
CBHW050444150626
46551CB00028B/1307